P9-DDZ-915

Fidget

BUSTERS

50 ways to keep kids busy while you get things done

DONNA BOZZO

The Countryman Press
A division of W. W. Norton & Company
Independent Publishers Since 1923

Contents

Introduction

Sure, you're a hands-on parent. But let's face it: Even the most hands-on parents among us still have times when they need to get things done.

I say that's when strategic play comes in—play you've anticipated and appropriately planned to help you create a quiet zone and carve out time to take that conference call, get the house ready for company, or give yourself a much-needed timeout. Imagine *that!* Or perhaps it's a welcome bag of tricks to store in your parenting arsenal to help you avoid those dreaded, can't-rewind-time moments when your child loses control. Think self-engaging games, fascinating activities, and hard-to-put-down toys you brilliantly have at the ready for those breaking moments when the kids just can't sit still one more minute, whether it's in the supermarket, the long car ride to Granny's, or a not-so-kid-friendly dinner. Or maybe it's not just reserved for 911 situations but a simple, everyday way to introduce mesmerizing play to fluff up the boring parts of your kids' routine.

I call all these wondrous secret weapons Fidget Busters. They are not only designed to keep kids' attention, but they also absorb the fidgety energy all kids inevitably have right at that moment you need them to *please sit still*. Nervous energy can run high when kids go somewhere unfamiliar, meet new people, or have to sit longer than their attention spans can handle. These Fidget Busters are designed to absorb all that squirming, grabbing, spilling, screaming energy—and head off meltdowns *before* they happen. I hope they will soon become your favorite tricks of the trade.

So what makes a good Fidget Buster? Well, for one, it has to grab your kids' attention while keeping them entranced and happily busy. I say your best go-to for that is sensory play, or what I call fun that rocks the senses. Sticky. Slippery. Gooey. Stretchy. Bumpy. Soft. Prickly. Spiny. Eye-popping. Simply-can't-put-down fun. Fidget-busting sensory toys feel so crazy good in little hands that kids can't stop touching, squishing, and spinning them. They can be squeezed super hard. They can be so soft or so scratchy you can't stop touching them. They can be turned over and around and upside down or cranked again and again to form a shape. They can be a puzzle that so tangles the mind, kids can't stop wanting to solve it. They can be newfangled or old-fashioned. Most importantly, unlike screens and electronic devices, you can hand these Fidget Busters over to your kids *guilt-free*.

And here's a bonus—many of these Fidget Busters help little ones develop fine motor skills and teach them about their surroundings. Fidget Busters give kids a chance to examine, discover, categorize, and make sense of the world around them. They provide all sorts of experiences that create a crucial foundation for more complex learning and behavior. Kids are really scientists discovering the world, and you create the lab with activities and toys that are so much fun you just might find yourself unable to put that new Fidget Buster down.

The Fidget Busters in This Book

This is a playbook of sorts—recommendations and recipes for tried and true Fidget Busters. Some you can buy. Some you and the kids can make at home. Some are both, meaning you can buy them, or make them depending on your schedule. I have to say, making them is my favorite way for sure because the fun isn't just in playing with the things you make. The planning and the making creates anticipation, learning, and warm memories. Plus, when kids create a Fidget Buster on their own, they become more invested in playing with it. *It's mine,* they'll say with pride.

This book is divided into chapters based on the best times for each activity. The Fidget Busters in the "On the Road & Running Errands" chapter are on the small and simple side. They can be easily toted, don't have a lot of parts, and promise to keep little hands and brains busy. "Dining Distractions" are more involved and meant to keep kids' hands and eyes engaged, so little ones stay sitting still longer. "Gimme a Minute" Fidget Busters make noise, bounce around, have parts, and are meant for play at home when you're trying to get stuff done—or just take a break. Finally, "Engrossingly Gross & Mesmerizingly Messy" Fidget Busters might be a little bit messy, but boy do they keep kids busy! Slimy, squishy, squeezy, gritty, your kids will LOVE these Fidget Busters. Just make sure they're in a mess-approved area before you let kids loose with this stuff. There is, of course, some crossover, and some Fidget Busters listed in "On the Road & Running Errands" are just as good for dinner parties or doing

Tip! You can bag or box up the materials needed for DIY Fidget Busters so they are ready for kids to make at a moment's notice, like when the phone rings or someone is at the door.

chores, so don't feel constrained by the chapters; they're just recommendations. Mix and match to your heart's content.

Stock up your kids' play area, your car, your bag—anywhere you can think of—with a variety of Fidget Busters so you'll always have something great on hand any time you need to keep kids busy. When one Fidget Buster gets boring, it's out with the old and in with the new—a more exciting toy for a busier quiet time. Fidget Busters create that guilt-free space in your day that allows you to tick a couple tasks off your list while the kids have some good clean fun.

A Commonsense Caution

The DIY projects in this book call for scissors, glue, tiny beads—craft supplies you probably already own. Only YOU can make the best call on whether or not your child can play with or make a Fidget Buster without supervision. I say children five and older can make most of the Fidget Busters in this book, and three is a good age to play with them. But you always know best. Also think safety when gathering supplies, and reach for tools like safety scissors and nontoxic glue—it can mean the difference between trying an activity and not. Small parts can be dangerous whether you are making or just playing with a Fidget Buster. This is especially true for magnets and magnetic toys, which can cause some very serious health issues. So use caution, and don't let kids under three play with them unsupervised. And, of course, always check age recommendations and warnings on store packaging.

On the
Road &
Running
Errands

Whether you're driving around, pushing a shopping cart, or waiting in line, all chores are easier when the kids in tow are quiet and happily absorbed. To pull off good behavior on the go, how about a bag of fidget-busting tricks to keep kids busy with something they can touch instead of knocking boxes off shelves, pulling clothes off racks, and getting into other mischief? The Fidget Busters in this chapter are all small, quiet, and self-contained, so you can take them just about anywhere to keep kids entertained while you get things done.

Fidget Spinner

  A three-armed plastic toy with a ball bearing in the center that spins easily.

Good Buy **Touch**

Who knew ball bearings—the key ingredient in the ultimate fidget-busting toy—could be so magical and create such a mania in the marketplace? That mystical, impossible-to-put-down motion somehow sucks us in, pulling out excess energy, unwanted nervousness, and boredom—a definite cure for the fidgets. In fact, you might want to pick one of these up for yourself and try it out the next time you're feeling a little anxious, because people claim that the soothing, engaging effects are just as good for adults as they are for children.

Kids can go beyond the spin with skill tricks, like balancing Fidget Spinners on their fingertips or passing them back and forth between their hands without stopping the spin. If you really want to keep kids still, challenge them to set records for tricks like longest fingertip spin. The prize? Another Fidget Buster! It's a win-win.

Fidget Snake

A slender mesh bag filled with marbles that can vary in color and size.

Good Buy

DIY

Touch

Small and easily stashed away, Fidget Snakes, homemade or store bought, can be just enough play to keep a kid's attention. The marbles against the netting creates a mesmerizing sensation as you flick the marbles back and forth.

DIY Directions

What You'll Need
narrow netting (available at craft stores)
marbles

Instructions
Roll the netting to create a tube. If you roll it so there are a few layers, then the marbles won't be able to escape. Tie one end of the netting tube and slide a few marbles into the tube. Tie the other end. Fidget away.

Glue on wiggle or googly eyes, crazy curly yarn hair, even red bumps or other decorations to give your Fidget Snakes extra texture and personality!

Fidget Ring

DIY **Touch** Beads are threaded on a key ring, allowing them to slip and slide but never spill.

Simple, flicky fun! With this Fidget Buster, there is extra fun in the making as you pick out the best colorful beads and make awesome designs. Since this is an activity that doesn't require cooking or chemicals, it's one older kids can happily do on their own.

DIY Directions

What You'll Need
beads
key ring

Instructions
Slide beads on the key ring for a handy Fidget Ring.

Add a little extra visual interest to your Fidget Rings by using unconventional beads. Play up your child's interests and look for beads in the shape of some of his or her favorites. Try hearts, stars, fish, or even baseballs. Or play up the holiday with pink and red beads for Valentine's Day, green for St. Patrick's Day, or orange and black for Halloween. Fidget Rings are also fun-to-make gifts!

Fidget Chain

Connected loops arranged so they flip and switch around, allowing for a variety of movements.

Good Buy   Touch

There are a number of different Fidget Chains out there. They look a little bit like bike parts and a lot like neon-colored fun. They softly jingle and jangle, with different parts that spin and flip, keeping hands busy as they twist them about. They might not spin like their fidget-busting brethren, but their parts roll smoothly for lots of tactile satisfaction.

Fidget Chains are great to have on hand for when you're on the go, as well as for quiet moments like when you're reading a story and trying to bring energy levels down for bedtime or nap time.

Whoosh Ball

Good Buy

DIY

Touch

Popular in the '80s, these "balls" are made with rubber strands that squish, tickle, and entertain.

Whoosh! **Just the sound makes this** Fidget Buster oh-so fun to squish and hold and pull and even make. You can buy a rubbery, spiny ball at any store, but you can also make them, and making them is a fun activity unto itself for kids. Just grab a couple handfuls of rubber bands and a pair of scissors for this fun, low-mess activity, and in a few pulls, ties, and snips, you're ready to play ball.

Keep your Whoosh Ball, or better yet Whoosh Balls, on hand for fast, distraction-free fun. They're great in the car or in a store, but they can do so much more. Whoosh Ball + friend = a game of toss. Whoosh Ball + an empty coffee container = a mini basketball game. Whoosh Ball + a few containers = a game of Bozo Buckets (rules can be easily found online). Whoosh Ball + an embroidery hoop = a game of aim. Fun to touch and hold, a Whoosh Ball is also great for solo toss and catch.

DIY Directions

What You'll Need
approximately 100
  rubber bands
scissors

Instructions
Start by stacking your
rubber bands, placing
them evenly one on top
of the other. Pick up the
stack, pinch the middle, and secure with a thick rubber band,
looping it around the stack a couple of times. Snip the loops of
each rubber band and *whoosh*.

Tip! Have kids pick the colors they want to use in their homemade Whoosh Ball one rubber band at a time. This will prolong the quiet time.

Squeezy Balloon

DIY

Touch

A balloon filled with rice, simple and surprisingly satisfying to squeeze.

Even grown-ups will get addicted to these. Squeezy Balloons are so great to have on hand to not only pass the time, but to give a reassuring squeeze during stressful moments like right before the big game. They are so easy to make and crazy inexpensive too. You may want to hand them out to the whole team!

Tie a piece of curling ribbon around the end for extra fanciness. Make a bundle in bright colors and keep them in a basket for a quick grab, or use them as party favors or gifts for friends.

DIY Directions

What You'll Need
balloons (however many you want)
rice
funnel

Instructions
Blow up the balloons several times to loosen them. Put the funnel in the opening and slowly pour the rice through the funnel until it's firmly packed. You may need to give the balloon a couple little shakes as the rice fills it up. Tie the end closed for fun fidget play.

Stress Ball

Good Buy **DIY** **Touch**

A malleable ball that can be squeezed with abandon.

Similar to a Squeezy Balloon, a Stress Ball is a great way to alleviate stress and is quieter on the squeeze. They've been popular items in toy stores, doctor's offices, office desks, and as promotional gifts for years. You probably have one in a drawer somewhere right now. If you don't, fear not, you can make them in a flash.

DIY Directions

What You'll Need
small, round balloon
funnel
1 cup cornstarch

Instructions

Blow up the balloon a few times to loosen it. Blow it up again until it's about 5 inches around. Place a funnel inside the opening and quickly pour the cornstarch into the funnel until the balloon is filled to about 3 inches in diameter. You might need to tap the funnel or stir the cornstarch occasionally to keep it moving into the balloon.

Pull up tightly on the opening of the balloon and pinch out any extra air.

Tie the balloon closed as near to the cornstarch as you can.

Tip! Having a helper makes this project much easier. Have someone hold the funnel and balloon while you pour the cornstarch.

For a looser Stress Ball, use fine play sand or split peas for the filler.

Pull a second balloon over the Stress Ball if your balloon seems thin and at risk of breaking.

Squishy- Swishy Goo Bags

Good Buy

DIY

Touch

Super-sealed sandwich bags filled with thick, gluey liquids.

Bright ooo-ooooo-oooozin' goo. These are oh-so-fun for kids to squeeze, run their fingers across, and even put up against their cheeks for a cool touch. The beads add an extra tactile and distracting element, as kids can trace and track beads through the goo for focused, anti-fidgety fun. You can buy these, usually in tube form, but they're so easy to make that they're worth creating on your own.

Find a theme that strikes your child's fancy for even more focused fun. Instead of beads, use plastic fish in a bag of blue goo for little marine biologists. Miniature cars are perfect for racing fans. Try plastic stars and a sun for out-of-this-galaxy play.

Squishy-Swishy Goo Bags are also handy for on-the-go fidget busting. Slide them into the back of car seats or slip them into toddler bags, and you have yourself an arsenal of fun.

DIY Directions

What You'll Need
1 cup cornstarch
⅓ cup sugar
4 cups cold water
few drops food coloring or
    water-soluble color tablet
wooden beads
zipper sandwich bags
glue (optional)

Instructions
Whisk together cornstarch, sugar, and water in a saucepan over medium heat until the mixture thickens and eventually solidifies. When it looks like goo or Vaseline, remove it from the heat. Mix in the food coloring. When it cools, pour the goo into a zipper sandwich bag along with the wooden beads. Seal shut with glue for children under five. Double bag it in another sandwich bag to prevent tears and spills.

No-Cook Variation
Because this recipe involves cooking, it will always involve some parent time in the making. But here's a shortcut! Skip the stove and pick up a tube of colorful hair gel instead. You get the same oooo-ooo goo, but this recipe saves on clean-up time.

Worry Doll

Good Buy

DIY

Touch

Sight

Little human figurines that will take on your worries for you.

I remember getting an assortment of adorable Worry Dolls at a funky store in the mall when I was a kid. They came with a little slip of paper that said to put all your worries into the doll, slip them under your pillow, and while you sleep the dolls will take your worries away. The funny thing is—if you believe it, it's true!

Worry Dolls are fun to have, hold, and carry around with you to whisk your worries away! And if you want to go the DIY route, kids will get totally absorbed in the process of creating their own little people with clothespins and scraps of fabric, yarn, string—whatever you can find around your house. Challenge them to make ones that look like their buddies, themselves, or their favorite star. Create a community of clothespin dolls and you'll always have a friend to hold on to.

DIY Directions

What You'll Need
clothespins
scraps of fabric, lace, and other textiles
yarn
glue
markers

Instructions
Make clothespins into
dolls by gluing on fabric
for clothes and yarn for hair.
Draw on eyes and mouths.

Have the kids create a fun spot for their community of Worry
Dolls. Retired boxes of any size make great little houses
that can be decorated with craft scraps. Felt makes great
carpeting, popsicle sticks make window frames, fabric can be
used for drapes, and cardboard jewelry boxes can be used as
simple furniture.

Worry Beads

DIY

Touch

A string of beads you can easily make with crafting odds and ends.

Count your worries away on a cord. Worry Beads are fun to thread and carry along for comfort in stressful moments, or they are just enough play to keep one's attention.

DIY Directions

What You'll Need
large beads
piece of cord or rope about 6 inches long

Instructions
Thread the beads on the cord or rope. Tie each end with a knot big enough that the beads don't slip off.

You can also tie the ends together to make a clacking loop of Worry Beads that can be slipped on as a bracelet so kids won't have to be without their beads when you're on the go.

Sticky Toys and Strips

Nylon or polyester fabric loops and hooks that stick together and tear apart with a very satisfying sound.

 Good Buy

 Hear

 Touch

Lots of toys come with loop-and-hook fasteners: stuffed animals, plushy books, and many baby toys are riddled with the stuff, and for good reason! The sound that they make as pieces pull away is tremendously satisfying. Sticking things back together is gratifying as well. For older kids, even simple hook-and-loop strips can absorb excess energy as the pieces are ripped apart and smushed back together. Look for ball toss sets to keep kids on the ball!

Hook-and-loop strips can be attached into circles and linked together to make chains of destructible decor. This is a great activity to give to kids who like having a goal when they play, or it can be a counting chain for an anticipated event like spring break!

Squeeze Ring

DIY

Touch

A slice of a foam pool (a.k.a. swim) noodle to squeeze the ever-loving heck out of.

Easy-peasy to make for pinchable, portable fun.
The fluffy texture that fits right in your hand squeezes out boredom, so independent playtime goes by swimmingly. And if your kids are old enough to use scissors, this is a safe activity for them to try on their own.

DIY Directions

What You'll Need
pool noodle
scissors

Instructions
Cut a swim noodle into pieces. Now squeeeeeeeeeeeze.

> The kids love squeezing, squishing, and smushing swim noodles, which you can get for oh-so cheap at a dollar store. Plus the twisty idea of using a pool toy indoors will be an added delight!

Stretchy String

Plastic, somewhat tacky strings that feel sticky but don't leave a residue.

 Good Buy

 Touch

Super snappy stretchy fun, these seemingly simple strings can stretch the time that drags between bath time and dinnertime. So fun to touch and hard to put down (that means you too, Mom), they come in *very* affordable packs of at least a dozen at party stores, toy stores, and lots of places online. This makes them almost worry-free disposable fun—really the best kind!

Go wild! If you want a little more personality for this Fidget Buster, look for fun animals made with the same silly string for your little zookeeper. Some even light up when whacked!

Oh-So-Soft-and-Scratchy Sensory Sticks

DIY **Touch**

Wooden sticks covered in textured materials that are pleasing to the touch.

Kids will get on the stick and stay on task decorating and playing with Sensory Sticks with fun-to-touch textures.

DIY Directions

What You'll Need
large popsicle sticks or paint stirrers
strips of sensory-rich material such as sandpaper, satin ribbon,
     rough fabric, a towel, cotton balls, soft baby blanket, felt

Instructions
Cut materials to fit popsicle sticks
or stirrers. Glue each item on
one side of each stick. Or mix
and match for even more
mesmerizing fun by gluing
sensory opposites (fuzzy and
gritty, bumpy and smooth) side
to side.

You can make Sensory
Sticks in every color of
the rainbow to add an
interesting visual element
to tactile play.

Dining
≈ Distractions

Whether you're at a restaurant, hosting a dinner party, or just eating a casual family meal, having an arsenal of Fidget Busters at the ready can turn a loud, squirmy, and—let's face it—whiny ordeal into a relaxed dining experience. Being able to keep kids' hands and eyes busy with something other than a screen may seem like an impossible fantasy, but this chapter will prove that dreams really can come true.

From classic books to puzzles in a bottle, there are loads of things you can give kids to keep them quietly occupied. They may even let you sneak in a bite or two of a new food or previously despised vegetable.

Quiet Book

 Good Buy   DIY   Touch   Sight

A homemade "book" featuring fun-to-touch tactile objects on each page.

You'll write the book on nonfidgety fun with Quiet Books filled with puffy, fluffy, scratchy, shiny, tacky, fun-touchy, and otherwise engaging pages that are great for keeping kids occupied on many levels. And occupied means quiet! Nonreaders will like playing Big Kid with a book they can *read* all on their own!

You can buy these, but they're usually aimed at babies. If you want to keep older kids' attention, it pays to "write" the book yourself or, better yet, have the kids create one. When it's personalized like that, they'll spend tons of time pouring over it at meals, and you'll get to eat in peace! This is a Fidget Buster even small kids can make on their own. In fact, you can put aside lots of puffy, fluffy, clippy, feely items and let them create their own library.

DIY Directions

What You'll Need

a blank wooden notebook
    (available on Amazon) or scrapbook
fun-to-touch items like buttons, cotton balls,
    googly eyes, paper clips, or beads
glue (or paste for younger kids)

Instructions

Glue fun-to-touch items onto each page.

You can keep a library of Quiet Books wherever your family has downtime. Ask kids to invent stories for the different textures. Maybe it's a story about goose bumps, prickly porcupines, or sleeping on a cloud. Let their imaginations run wild!

Falling, Falling Beads Bottle

Good Buy **DIY** **Sight** — A hypnotizing bottle filled with beads that fall through thick liquid in a slow, meandering motion.

Beads cascade through a clear, dense mixture, creating a mesmerizing, calming experience that goes great with dinner. Some beads fall slower, some faster, but all in lackadaisical fashion as a bright parade swims past kids' eyes. As the last one falls, they won't be able to resist tipping the bottle over and back again to watch them all drift by in random design. You can buy lots of versions of a Falling, Falling Beads Bottle, but they're so-so super fun and easy to make, you might as well try one at home.

DIY Directions

What You'll Need

1-liter bottle with cap (a
   VOSS water bottle
   works very well)
3 bottles clear hand soap
3 tablespoons clear dish
   soap
colored plastic beads
glue

Tip! If you use more dish soap, your beads will fall more rapidly. If you use more of the thicker hand soap, the beads will fall more slowly.

Instructions

Fill the bottle with both soaps. Add plastic beads. It's a good idea to glue on the lid.

So pretty to watch, keep your Falling, Falling Beads Bottle by a window. Coordinate colors for special events and holidays, like red and green for Christmastime or orange and black for Halloween.

Hidden Picture Book

**Good
Buy**

Sight

Interactive books that hide common
objects among busy scenery, effectively
creating a one-player game.

Is there anything more absorbing than a busy scene filled with
laughing animals, profusions of flowers, some crashing waves . . .
and plenty of hidden silly objects? People, no matter what age,
usually can't put down a Hidden Picture Book until they find
every last dang item they're looking for. And the silly absurdity
of a broom mustache on the moon, a spatula for a cat's tail, and
a frying pan in a flower is extra delightful for kids.

There are a million of these books on the market. You can
get them in workbook form, which allows kids to color in the
objects as they find them, or you can buy gorgeous hardcovers
that enchant young eyes with their amazing art. No matter
what kind you buy, you really can't go wrong with these quiet-
inducing tableside companions.

If young eyes get frustrated looking for hidden objects, turn
the book upside down or sideways. This unexpected twist can
reengage kids and help them rethink the page.

Ocean Bottle

A lava-lampesque bottle of liquid that just looks really super cool.

Good Buy

DIY

Sight

Kids will be completely enchanted watching the deep blue ocean waves rock back and forth. This Fidget Buster is easy for older kids to create on their own. Just collect the supplies and set them aside for that long family dinner with the in-laws and set the fidgets out to sea.

DIY Directions

What You'll Need
1-liter bottle with cap
funnel
mineral oil
blue food coloring or
    water-soluble color tablet
glue

For extra fun, add colorful plastic fish, glitter, or even some small shells. You can also make this a Lava Bottle using red or orange food coloring or a Slime Bottle using green food coloring.

Instructions
Fill bottle almost halfway with mineral oil. Add a few drops of blue food coloring. Fill the bottle the rest of the way with water. Glue on cap. Shake the bottle to mix.

Zigzag Bag

DIY **Touch** A sealed bag of squishy lotion kids can trace their fingers on for the sensation of making a mess without the actual mess.

This squishy bag is a little bit game, a little bit sensory satisfaction. It's also strategically discreet and magically distracting, making it a great dining companion for squirmy, can't-sit-still kids.

DIY Directions

What You'll Need
2 clear sandwich bags
black marker
baby lotion
glue (optional)

If zigzags aren't your kid's thing, draw spirals, triangles, or other shapes. Artsy? Try drawing animals, mazes, even little scenes like the Three Little Pigs. Make many bags and swap them out over your sealed inner bag of gluey goo.

Instructions
Turn one bag inside out and draw zigzags on it. Allow to dry. Turn the bag right side out, put the second bag inside it, and fill the inner bag with lotion. Seal the inner bag, gluing it shut if desired. Zip the outer bag closed. You can also glue that one shut if desired. Have kids trace and retrace the zigzags with their fingers.

Magical Colors Bag

A sealed bag of foamy colors that mix together to create new colors right before kids' eyes.

DIY   Touch   Sight

Kids won't be able to get enough of watching new colors emerge as they mix up the squishy components of this Fidget Buster. And it's a lot more fun to watch them play with this than their food!

DIY Directions

What You'll Need
shaving cream
tempera paint
gallon-sized zipper plastic bags
glue (optional)

> You can also lay the Magical Colors Bag flat and have kids draw pictures, letters, or designs with their fingers.

Instructions
Add a lot of shaving cream to the bags, then add two primary paint colors to each.

Squeeze the extra air out of the bags and zip shut, gluing them sealed for smaller kids.

Have kids squish and squeeze the bags so they can watch the colors mush into each other, forming new colors.

Hidden Treasure Bottle

DIY **Sight** **Touch**

Filled with lots of rice and a few little toys, this bottle hides the goods so kids keep on turning it and turning it to find them.

I spy with my little eye . . . a clever twist on the classic car game. These bottles are so much fun to shake and discover the treasures hidden inside—perfect for any place and time you need to bust some fidgeting.

DIY Directions

What You'll Need
clear bottle with cap
enough rice to fill it
small treasures such as plastic
 toys, coins, or bright pencil
 erasers
glue

Tip! You can also use sand or dried beans in place of rice.

Instructions

Pour rice inside bottle, stopping occasionally to put in items. Almost fill it up, leaving just enough wiggle room for the rice. Glue the cap on.

Kids can shake, turn, and rotate to discover the hidden treasures.

Pick a theme. Choose the treasures based on a vacation destination or your child's favorite hobby, such as dinosaurs for little paleontologists.

Kaleidoscope

Good Buy   DIY   Sight

A tunnel of shapes and light that was first invented as far back as the sixteenth century.

Eye candy! Do you remember the first time you were completely entranced by a kaleidoscope? These classic toys are so engrossing because they seem to explode and evolve endlessly. As you twist and turn them, their beauty blooms and changes, which can captivate visual kids for a surprisingly long time—sometimes long enough to survive a sibling's loooong, boring soccer car pool!

DIY Directions

What You'll Need

empty Pringles can with lid

hammer and nail

silver holographic paper

tape

clear plastic paper (like you'd find in a scrapbook)

contact paper, gift wrap, or any kind of paper to decorate outside of can

plastic gemstones or colored sequins

Instructions

Hammer an eyehole in bottom of the empty Pringles can and line the inside of the can with holographic paper. Tape to secure. Decorate outside of the can.

Glue plastic gemstones or sequins to the inside of the lid. Trace the lid on a piece of clear plastic paper and cut the resulting circle. Tape it in place over the gemstones or sequins. Place lid on can. Aim toward light, look through the peephole, and twist the kaleidoscope for beautiful vistas.

Shortcut

Rather than hunting down supplies around the house, look for kits online that come with everything you need to make your own kaleidoscope.

Masterpiece! Add a coloring component to kaleidoscope adventures by giving kids crayons and paper and asking them to draw what they see down the barrel of this Fidget Buster—fireworks, glowing globs, marching ants. The artistic possibilities are as boundless as the kaleidoscopic visions.

Cube Puzzle

Good Buy

Brain

Touch

A cube-shaped toy with a puzzle element that has kids match colors or dismantle the cube and reassemble it.

Twisty, tricky turnkey fun! Cube quiet time and curb the fidgets with classic Cube Puzzles. What I like about these all-time favorite Fidget Busters is they tickle the brain and are quiet and compact, making them an instant remedy for uninvited silliness or chronic boredom. Just tuck in a tote or pocket for fidget busting on the go. They are also addictive—I mean who can put down a Rubik's Cube without one more last twisty, turny crank? Of course this classic puzzle is pretty advanced, but for some kids that means it'll keep their attention indefinitely. If you think it'll cause more frustration than fidget busting, simpler cube toys with less squares, like Snake Cube, which unravels into long strings of shapes and back again, might be a better fidget fit.

Old, worn-out Cube Puzzles can be revitalized with new stickers. Just make sure you (or your kids) match the same kind of sticker with each color and you can have a customized, flower-themed, car-crazy, or doggy-adorable puzzle.

Tangle Toy

Interconnected tube pieces that can be moved around and manipulated in countless directions. Many allow for pieces to be added or taken away.

Good Buy

Touch

Colorful, great for lots of ages, and utterly addictive, Tangle Toys have it all! They are classic Fidget Busters, as they are so satisfying to turn and tangle and twist, keeping hands busy, busy, busy! And they therefore keep kids calm and their minds relaxed. You might have to airplane in some bits of food when your kid really gets into a tangle with this toy!

Do you have any hand issues like stiffness or limited mobility? If you do, you might want to consider picking up a Tangle Toy for yourself, as their twisting, turning actions are great exercise to strengthen and stretch hands, which can restore mobility and generally help rehabilitate injured mitts.

Gimme a

Minute

Sometimes you just need a minute. A minute to make a call, fold some laundry, do the dishes, or just sit and zone out on your phone. Don't tell the kids! These Fidget Busters help you grab some quiet time throughout your day by distracting kids with independent play. The toys in this chapter sprawl out a bit more, so they're great for when kids are home in their play area or room. They may not be as quiet or contained as some of the other Fidget Busters, but they make up for that by being so fun and so distracting that they keep kids entertained longer.

Super Bouncy Ball

Good Buy   DIY   Touch

Just the most classic toy in all of kiddom!

Put some bounce in those dull moments and distract kids with a Super Bouncy Ball. It's amazing how long children will chase a wildly bouncing ball!

If you ask me, homemade Super Bouncy Balls are even better than the store-bought item for a few reasons, one of which is that they are fun to make because the process is so interesting! Little science lovers will love this gloopy, gloppy, rolling recipe. (They're easy for kids to make on their own, if you don't mind the creative mess.) And since they won't be the perfect spheres you get from the store, their bounce can be really erratic, sending them sideways (boing!), which means more giggle fun for little ones.

DIY Directions

What You'll Need
3 tablespoons cornstarch
3 tablespoons plus
     1 ½ teaspoons water
couple drops of food
     coloring or water-
     soluble color tablet

Tip! Invest in a set of jacks to soup up the Super Bouncy Ball play and get ready for mesmerizing fun that builds focus and hand-eye coordination.

Instructions

Mix cornstarch, water, and coloring in a microwave-safe bowl. It'll be a bit hard to stir, but once combined, microwave the mixture for 20 seconds. Add 1½ teaspoons of water and mix. Peel the mixture out of the bowl and knead together, rolling the mixture in your hands to form a ball. Microwave the ball for 20 seconds and let cool.

Start a collection! Super Bouncy Balls make a super collection. Display them in tall acrylic or glass vases. The bright colors combine for a sight-sensory explosion. My 18 year old has been collecting since she was five!

Hippity-Hop Balls

Good Buy **Touch**

Part ball, part ride, these big rubber beauties with handles are ridden by kids who have some energy to bounce out.

Want to take bouncy ball play to a HUGE next level? Then get your kids that energy-burning, fidget-busting, can't-stop-going classic, the Hippity-Hop Ball. This was my favorite toy as a kid. I remember bounding and bouncing up and down the driveway for hours. I love this Fidget Buster because it makes kids move. I'm not sure if you remember how much oomph it takes to bounce around on these oversized bouncy balls with handles, but it's A LOT. Hopping around on these things is sure to cause fits of giggling that make time fly for the kids and earn you some much-needed getting-things-done time.

Trying to keep more than one kid busy? A Hippity-Hop Ball race is sure to keep 'em going on their own. Anyone for best two out of three? How about three out of five? How about blindfolded? One-handed?

Rain Maker

A tube that tinkles when turned over as dried grains fall against the pegs inside.

 Good Buy

 DIY

 Hear

 Touch

Nothing is more mesmerizing than the sound of rain. Skip the store, grab some toothpicks, grains, and a couple retired chopsticks to make the ultimate homemade sound machine.

DIY Directions

What You'll Need
clear plastic bottle with cap
box of toothpicks
a couple of dowel rods or chopsticks

small, uncooked grains like quinoa or rice
glue (optional)

Instructions
Drop the toothpicks into the bottle so they land vertically. Drop the dowel rods or chopsticks into the bottle. Add grains. Screw on cap, gluing it on if desired for younger kids, and turn.

Paint your grains in rainbow, neon, or glow-in-the-dark colors (and allow to dry) to make this project visually engaging as well as pleasing to the ear.

GIMME A MINUTE

Distracting Dice

Good Buy | DIY | Brain | Touch

Whether store-bought or homemade to add a touch component, dice are classic time takers that give kids a math edge.

I just love dice! They are the ultimate when it comes to killing time. Plus, they keep little (and big) brains blossoming if you use them to play a math game. So why not make some of your own dice to keep the good times rolling?

I keep a handful of dice just about everywhere. There's a bag of them in the console of my Suburban, a jar of them on our kitchen island and on our bar top in the basement, and I have a handful in the zipped compartment of my purse. With dice, the kids always have a game on hand. Just practicing your "rolls" is addicting. Introduce them to simple math games. Roll and subtract. Roll and add. Roll for doubles—how many can you get?

DIY Directions

What You'll Need
cube-shaped box or Styrofoam cube
wiggle or googly eyes, circle-shaped stickers, or beads

Instructions
Glue shapes onto each side
of your cube to mimic dice
and you're ready to roll!

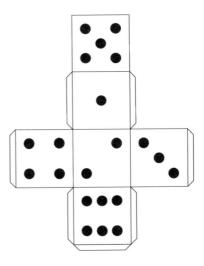

Magnetic Mr. Funny Faces

   🖐

Good Buy   **DIY**   **Brain**   **Touch**

A homemade take on the beloved Mr. Potato Head.

Who doesn't remember Mr. Potato Head and hours of arranging and rearranging mister's face for funny fun? Re-create that irresistible retro play DIY-style with some retired vegetable or soup cans and small household items.

Tip! Challenge the kids to a Funny–Face Off! Have them make their best faces and post them on social media or text them to family members for votes.

Keep play interesting by introducing new shapes from time to time. Anything works! Try clothespins for a nose, quarters or old poker chips for ears, plastic flower petals for lips, retired sunglasses, foam curlers, Christmas garlands, mismatched earrings . . .

DIY Directions

What You'll Need

large cans (coffee cans with
    lids make for lots of storage)
duct tape
felt
large wiggle or googly eyes
ping-pong balls
black Sharpie
adhesive magnetic tape in tabs or strips

Instructions

Line inside rim of can with duct tape to hide sharp edge. Cut out felt shapes for your Magnetic Mr. Funny Faces—ears, mustaches, noses. Use large googly eyes or ping-pong balls with black circles drawn on for eyes. Or get creative and use retired Legos, beads, plastic forks, and more for fun features. Stick magnetic strips or tabs on the back of each shape. Arrange and rearrange!

Magnets can be very dangerous if swallowed and must not be used unsupervised by children age three or younger. Please keep that in mind when considering this or any other magnetic toy for your child.

Skill Shot Ball Toss

DIF

Brain   Touch

An easy game, similar to cornhole, that keeps kids trying over and over to throw balls into holes.

You can pull out all the stops with a little court time whenever you need a time-out! Simple, inexpensive, and fun to make, this homemade ball toss really is a great activity for kids—and the decorating is half the fun. Skill Shot Ball Toss is also a great game to keep squirmy players' eyes on the ball whenever you need to blow the whistle and create a time-out for yourself.

DIY Directions

What You'll Need
a can with a plastic lid (a Pringles can works great)
ping-pong balls
paper and glue, or adhesive shelf liner
markers, glitter, beads, and craft shapes for decorating
scissors

Instructions
Draw a circle on the plastic lid that is slightly bigger than a ping-pong ball. Cut out the circle with scissors. Decorate the can with paper, markers, beads, glitter, and shapes.

Gameplay
The object of the game is to toss the ball in the can. Kids can take turns trying, keep trying until they make it, use a three-strikes-you're-out policy, or whatever other system works for them.

Take play to the pro level! Decorate containers with stickers or duct tape stamped with your favorite professional sports team logos. Complete the look with sporty foam shapes.

Gone Fishing

☑️ Good Buy   ✂️ DIY   🧠 Brain   👁️ Sight

A cute way to spend some time using a magnet on string to catch some felt fish hiding magnets of their own.

Get them fishing instead of fidgeting! This Fidget Buster requires concentration—which means quiet time for you! You can buy magnetic fishing games at most toy stores, but if you're not into yet another battery-operated piece of plastic, the homemade version of this activity is even better than the prefab one. Older kids can definitely make this one on their own. For the little ones, you will need to set it up in advance for ongoing fishy fun. When it gets quiet and you wonder what they've been up to, you'll realize they've gone, gone, Gone Fishing!

There are always more fish in the sea! Change up fishing play with other sea creatures: an octopus, a shark, or a starfish. Creating new oceans for them to explore will keep your kids busy for a long, long time.

DIY Directions

What You'll Need

colorful felt

cotton stuffing

thread or embroidery floss

needle

zinc-plated fender washers
(available at hardware
stores)

twine or string

dowel rod, branch,
chopstick, wooden knitting needle, or drum
stick for mini fishing pole

scissors

magnet

mini wiggle or googly eyes

ribbon bits

Magnets can be very
dangerous if swallowed
and must not be used
unsupervised by children
age three or younger.
Please keep that in mind
when considering this or
any other magnetic toy for
your child.

Instructions

Draw fish shapes on pieces of felt folded in half. Cut out
shapes. Sew back to front, leaving space for stuffing. Stuff
each felt fish with zinc-plated fender washers and cotton
stuffing. Finish stitching the fish. Glue on mini wiggle or
googly eyes and ribbon for scales.

Tie twine to your fishing pole. Tie the magnet to the
other end of the twine, and it's fishing time.

Finger Worms and Puppets

| Good Buy | DIY | Brain | Touch | Sight |

A great way to get second life out of some old gloves is to turn them into actors for their own kiddie theater.

Ten fingers can put on a 10-star show with DIY Finger Worms. Easy to find in stores or online but even more fun to make, Finger Worms and Puppets equal loads of independent play. Little ones can even be put in charge of creating this item. For younger finger-puppet playgoers whom you don't trust with scissors, just cut the fingers off the gloves beforehand.

Lights, camera, action! Challenge kids to prepare and present a Finger Puppet play. A retired shoebox draped with a piece of felt makes the perfect Finger Puppet stage. Record it with your phone for fun playback. Text to Grandma—a homemade Netflix!

DIY Directions

What You'll Need
retired gloves
pieces of felt and fabric
scraps of ribbon, beads, yarn
mini wiggle or googly eyes
glue

Instructions
Cut the fingertips off
gloves at about the
knuckle. Make into finger
puppets by gluing on
scraps of felt, fabric,
ribbons, beads, googly
eyes, and yarn for hair.

Tip! Kids can take the show on the road, meaning this Fidget Buster is also good for errands . . . if you don't mind losing a few pieces in the supermarket or dentist's waiting room.

Tapping Keys

DIY   **Hear**

A wind chime made of upcycled keys that unlock who-knows-what.

Like the twinkling of piano keys, the spontaneous medley of windblown keys calms the senses. Plus it's such a fun activity to do together or set up for children old enough to work on their own.

DIY Directions

What You'll Need
retired keys

paints and paintbrush

twine or yarn

small branch or dowel rod

Instructions
Paint keys. When dry, tie each onto a piece of twine, all the same length. Then tie the other end of the twine onto the branch so the keys hang a couple inches apart from one another. Tie a piece of twine from one end of the branch to the other with enough give to form a hanger. Hang outside to let the wind work its magic or inside and tap for whispers of sound.

You can add beaded lengths of twine, craft feathers, or other leftover craft supplies to up the visual elements.

Maracas

Instruments that are essentially big rattles for big kids.

Good Buy

DIY

Hear

Touch

We are now firmly in the land of really fun but pretty raucous fidget busting. But what you trade in quiet you get back in independent fun! Maracas are great for getting out the too-much-candy shakes or the overstimulated tantrum. Kids can take all their buzzing energy and shake it out with all their might. Who knows, they might even shake it to the beat once in a while!

DIY Directions

What You'll Need
homemade Egg Shakers
(see page 66)
sticks
tape
stickers or paint

Play your favorite tunes and ask kids to play along with their Maracas. This can be a really captivating challenge if kids get into the groove.

Instructions
Tape sticks onto homemade Egg Shakers, decorate them, and you've got DIY Maracas!

Egg Shaker

Good Buy | DIY | Touch | Hear

A little piece of the rhythm section that uses dried grains or other small objects as sound makers inside a plastic egg shell.

Shake, shake, shake, rattle, and roll! Add zest to those dull moments with an Egg Shaker. Creating them at home is not just for Eastertime, as these crazy-easy-to-make Fidget Busters will spice up any dull times. Dance. Sing. And make some noise! Which, granted, may not be quiet fidget busting, but it's definitely a fun distraction to get the fidgets out of their system. Especially if you can manage to get the parade to head outside.

DIY Directions

What You'll Need
plastic Easter eggs
beans, small grains, dried peas, or beads
glue

Instructions
Open your plastic Easter egg so the two pieces are separated.
Pour beans, small grains, dried peas, or beads into the bottom
half of the egg, filling it almost to the rim. Glue the two pieces
together. Wipe away excess glue.

Shake up the sound by experimenting with different fillers.
Try marbles, small erasers (for a quieter version), jingle bells,
or whatever is handy at home.

Tambourine

Good Buy   **DIY**   **Hear**

Disks that have little cymbals around the edges and sometimes a drumhead on one surface of the disk. Also, a noise riot.

Tambourines are flashy. They're grown-up. They're real instruments. And they're *really* loud. That's why kids can't keep their hands off them. They want to shake them for their cymbal-crashing cacophony. They want to dance with them. They want to use them as a steering wheel when they drive the bus. They want to drop them on the ground to listen to the explosive sounds they make. This is all great if you're looking for independent play but not necessarily a whole lot of quiet.

Take the Maraca play-along challenge from page 65 to the next level. Turn on a beloved tune and challenge kids to play AND dance along. You'll probably want to get your camera out for this one, as the cuteness just doesn't quit.

Jingle Bells

The cheery sound of Jingle Bells doesn't have to be restricted to the holiday season!

Good Buy **Touch** **Hear**

OK, we're through the loudest of loud and back to some of the more enjoyable sounds. Jingle Bells have a uniquely pleasing and recognizable sound that kids (and adults) just love. Maybe it reminds some of them of Santa? That certainly couldn't hurt!

You can get Jingle Bells as lone bells, arranged on sticks, curved around a tambourine, on a hook-and-loop strip that can be fastened around wrists and ankles for a dance party, inside baby-proofed silicone toys, and in so many more setups. They're great for just about all ages and should be part of any musical fidget-busting arsenal.

Wearable Jingle Bells, such as the ones on hook-and-loop straps for wrists and ankles, provide the added bonus of letting you keep an ear on your kids.

Magnetic Marvels

 Good Buy   **Brain**   **Touch**

A type of toy made of magnets that can be manipulated and sculpted into endless shapes.

Magnets make for some amazing Fidget Busters. They come in a wide variety of toys that appeal to a wide variety of kids. Little ones can spend a surprising amount of time clicking and clacking magnetic blocks and tiles that snap into pleasing shapes and structures.

When kids get older and you can trust them not to eat toy pieces, a world of magnetic sculptures opens up. Blobs of magnetic balls that you can mash and mush and roll and push feel so cool to play with, and they can be used to create some really incredible objects. Or you can get magnetic stands

Make sure magnetic play is kept far away from electronic devices, as the magnets can damage certain kinds of screens and drives. Usually the magnets in toys are fairly weak and the risk is minimal—but better safe than sorry.

Magnets can be very dangerous if swallowed and must not be used unsupervised by children age three or younger. Please keep that in mind when considering this or any other magnetic toy for your child.

that support all sorts of shapes—stars, moons, hearts, dolphins, flowers, whatever you like—to create some really beautiful abstract sculptures. You'll probably want one of those for your own desk!

Good Ol' Coloring and Activity Books

Good Buy   **DIY**   **Brain**   **Sight**

One of the best outlets for creativity and energy ever imagined.

I recently attended a high school basketball game and spotted a pair of very young girls sitting next to each other, each completely immersed in an iPhone, neither watching the game or interacting with each other. A few rows down, I spotted two other little ones about the same age, drawing and laughing together, pointing at each other's papers. Next to them was a pack of crayons and a stack of paper a parent must have brought along. It doesn't have to be hard or expensive.

A pack of crayons and a workbook filled with mazes, puzzles, and coloring pages remain some of the best Fidget Busters out there. Every topic, every brand, every character, every everything pretty much has its own Activity Book. You can keep kids busy with their favorite animals or learning letters and numbers. They can go on undersea adventures, rocket into space, or explore distant lands—all while you get some peace and quiet.

DIY Directions

What You'll Need
two 8 x 10 pieces of
    poster board
paper
stapler, paper fasteners,
    or hole punch and
    string

Tip! Pick different themes like My Family, My Town, or My Favorite Holiday. DIY coloring books are great for slightly older children to make, but they're good for little ones too.

Instructions
Do you have inspiring artists? Challenge them to draw their own Activity Books on blank paper. Poster board stapled or tacked together with paper fasteners makes a nice cover, which they will love decorating. Or even punch holes on the side and tie together with string. Keep a few blank ones to take with you to places where you want to keep little inspired artists busy.

The coloring craze for adults means there are even more coloring books on the market today than ever before. If your kids seem like they're getting a little bored with the books aimed at children, you can reinvigorate their love of coloring by getting them some colored pencils (when they're ready) and a book marketed to adults. They'll love feeling like they're doing something grown-ups do. Maybe you can give them some tax forms next!

Buddha Board

Good Buy   Brain   Sight

A canvas kids can make designs on with nothing but water, then learn a bit about zen as their creations disappear.

Commonly known as a Buddha Board, this is a Fidget Buster that seems so sophisticated that kids will think they're getting away with something by playing with it. The concept is simple, though. You just dip a paintbrush in clean water and "paint" on the board. The design you create then disappears as it dries. How does it work? I don't know! A Buddha Board is made of magical (but also natural) materials. Kids will love creating pictures and then watching them slowly disappear, which really extends the amount of occupied time you get out of it! What's more zen than that?

You can get some pretty expensive and elegant-looking Buddha Boards. You can also get some that are affordable and come in neon colors. They are not indestructible, as the surface can scratch and become worn, so I recommend the latter version.

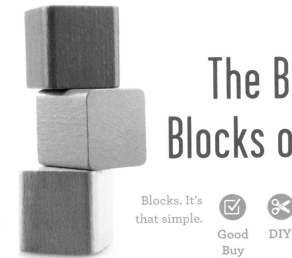

The Building Blocks of Quiet

Blocks. It's that simple.

Good Buy   DIY   Brain   Touch

Building is one of the most engrossing activities. You can get wood blocks, magnetic blocks, interolocking blocks, blocks that look like bricks, and even fuzzy or foamy blocks.

Things that can really get kids block crazy, and therefore out of your hair, are giant blocks. If you tape shut empty shoeboxes, cereal boxes, moving boxes, shipping boxes, and all the other boxes that inevitably pile up and seem to multiply in the garage, you have created massive blocks for kids to build with. They can even color or paint these to their hearts' content.

Odds are you have a lot of different Building Blocks and construction toys that don't officially go together. Challenge kids to intermix the different blocks they have to make new things. Get them to think outside the box! This can help get them reinterested in toys that may have fallen out of favor.

Glowing Nighttime Lantern

 Good Buy DIY Sight

A nightlight disguised as a lantern that has soft, twinkling light that soothes sleepy kids.

Any spot in your home becomes a campout with a Glowing Nighttime Lantern. You can find lots of lanterns made for kids, but they can be really fun to make and dreamy for kids to lie next to when it's time to wind down and let their thoughts drift away. Kids old enough to leave home (not really) might want to strike out for a walk around the block for a glowy dusk pajama walk.

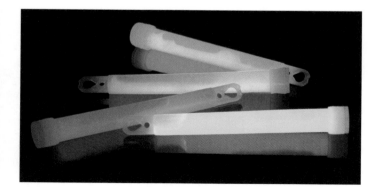

DIY Directions

What You'll Need
glow sticks
gloves (optional)
scissors
mason jars with lids, or
    plastic bottles with caps
    for younger kids
silver glitter
glue (optional)

Instructions
Crack a glow stick to
activate it. Put on the gloves.
Cut the clear ends of the glow stick off and empty the liquid
into the jar. Add water. Sprinkle in lots of silver glitter and let it
glow. Screw on the cap, gluing in place for younger kids.

For a brighter jar, add more than one glow stick. For best
results, use emergency glow sticks because they glow
brighter.

Engrossingly Gross & Mesmerizingly Messy

Some of the squishiest, stickiest, ickiest, messiest Fidget Busters are also the most effective at keeping little hands big-time busy. The projects in this chapter truly feel engrossingly gross. Kids (and maybe even you) won't be able to stop touching and squeezing and playing with them. While they are absolutely great at keeping kids entertained, be forewarned that this big dose of fun comes with a side of mess! Even playing with them can mean sticky business.

Kinetic Sand

Good Buy   **DIY**   **Touch**

Scupltable sand you've seen on display at the mall but can easily make at home.

You don't need the beach to make magic castles in the sand. With a batch of Kinetic Sand you can create a fantasy beach for random gray-day (or any-day) play. Magical, mystical, and colorful, Kinetic Sand is irresistibly gritty to the touch. And while it's become a popular toy store item, it's really fun and easy to make at home. The kids will beg to play Beach all day long.

DIY Directions

What You'll Need
1 cup very fine, white sand (available at craft stores)
1 tablespoon cornstarch
1 tablespoon fine glitter (gold, silver, or a color to match the color of the sand you're making)
1 tablespoon water, plus more for later
1 teaspoon dish soap
½ teaspoon food coloring or water-soluble color tablet

Give your kids shovels, cookie cutters, spoons, and even forks to use as fun molds. Store your Kinetic Sand in airtight bin for ongoing sensory play.

Instructions

Pour all the dry ingredients into a large bowl. Pour the wet ingredients into a smaller bowl. Mix each separately. Combine the ingredients from both bowls in the larger bowl. Mix. Then knead. Add additional water 1 tablespoon at a time until you get the consistency of sandcastle-making sand. You want it to be moist enough so you can build with it but not so wet it doesn't clump. You also don't want it to be so dry it doesn't hold together.

Rainbow Variation

Repeat to make other colors, and combine them to make rainbow sand.

Food coloring can stain clothes and fingers, so be sure to dress kids in play clothes for this one and consider giving them a pair of plastic gloves. Alternatively, you can leave the food coloring out altogether or use water-soluble color tablets that are meant for bath-time play.

Floam

Good Buy **DIY** **Touch**

Not quite foam, not quite clay, Floam is funnily textured, moldable stuff kids love.

Sticky + bumpy = hard to put down. You'll find sticky, squeezy, bumpy, poppy, stretchy, moldable, pinchable, blobbable fun in fabulous Floam. This is another "why buy?" for me, because you can make it so easily ahead of playtime or as an activity with kids.

DIY Directions

What You'll Need

1 six-ounce bottle of Elmer's glue in a fun color

½ tablespoon baking soda

¼ cup water

1½ tablespoons saline solution

½ cup polystyrene beads or beanbag filler

Tip! You can get polystyrene beads and beanbag filler at most dollar stores.

Instructions

Pour the glue into a bowl. Add the baking soda and water. Slowly add the saline solution a few teaspoons at a time, mixing in between. Mix and then knead, adding more saline solution if needed. Add beads, and knead until fully mixed.

Floam is the perfect thing to hand off when you have to take a work call at home. And it's good for fun on the run. Pack DIY Floam in zipper sandwich bags for Floam fun on that next long car trip or a day of endless errands.

Crackle Foam

DIY **Touch** Thick foam, with a little extra pop, that can be molded, sculpted, or just squished through little fingers.

Crackle Foam not only tingles the touch senses, but the crackling of the Pop Rocks creates sound sensory fun too.

DIY Directions

What You'll Need
1 cup cornstarch
1 cup shaving cream
1 packet Pop Rocks candy

Tip! Pick up extra Pop Rocks candy for a sensational sensory treat. Or leave out the candy altogether for smooth foam.

Instructions
Mix equal amounts of cornstarch and shaving cream until you form a moldable foam dough. Add the Pop Rocks candy for crackling fun.

You can make as much or as little of this Fidget Buster as you like, as long as you use a 1:1 ratio of cornstarch to shaving cream.

Silly Putty

A fun little lump of malleable . . . stuff. While you don't know what's in the store-bought, you can be sure the homemade version is purely organic.

Good Buy

DIY

Touch

While store-bought Silly Putty is made with who-knows-what, you can leave little ones alone with the homemade version of this Fidget Buster, because there are only two ingredients, and they are both edible (though not tasty when combined).

DIY Directions

What You'll Need
1 cup yogurt
1 ½ cups corn starch

Instructions
Mix yogurt and cornstarch well until putty starts to form. Knead until you like the consistency.

> For play later in the day or week, refrigerate this fidget-busting putty in an airtight container. This will preserve it for curious play for a couple days.

Distractabin

Good Buy

DIY

🖐 **Touch**

A kitchen basin or other little tub filled with dried beans that hide away fun little toys that kids have to "dig" for with their hands.

Burying treasure in a bin of sensory-satisfying dried beans will keep little hands happily digging and burying treasure again and again. You can get these at stores, but they're exceptionally easy to put together yourself.

DIY Directions

What You'll Need
bin (a dishwashing bin from a dollar store works great)
enough dried beans to almost fill the bin
plastic toys or other items that will be fun to dig for

Instructions
Fill a bin with dried beans. Bury fun-to-touch items like plastic toys inside.

Provide sand shovels or scoops to give little hands something extra to dig with. While these aren't as tactile as digging with your hands, the sound of the plastic shoveling through the beans is a great sensory experience.

Squishy Snow

A foam imitation of every kid's favorite winter toy: snow minus the cold temperature and dreaded melt.

 DIY

 Touch

Who needs winter for snowman fun? Declare a snow day and give your kids everything they need to create their own fun storm of snow. The smooth texture and the sharp smell will tingle their senses, and the time it takes them to make and play will free you up for chores or, better yet, a little R&R.

DIY Directions

What You'll Need
1 cup baking soda
shaving cream
a few drops peppermint oil or
    extract
a few shakes white or silver
    glitter

Twigs for arms, felt for a hat, an orange bead for a nose, and retired snaps for buttons make a Squishy Snow snowman come alive.

Instructions
Pour baking soda in a bowl and add shaving cream slowly until you get a snowy consistency. Add peppermint and glitter for extra sparkle and scent.

Playdough

Good Buy

DIY

🤚 **Touch**

A reusable, nondrying, stiff dough that can be sculpted or just squished.

Break out some Playdough and kids become busy as bees. They can squish, squeeze, and mold Playdough for hours, scooping, rolling, and building whatever they like. I find homemade Playdough is even better than store bought. It's softer, stretchier, and even more irresistible if you add some cool scents.

DIY Directions

What You'll Need

1 cup flour
½ cup salt
2 teaspoons cream of tartar
1 cup water or cooled tea (for its scent)
1 ½ tablespoons oil
food coloring or water-soluble color tablet
essential oils, spices, or flavor extracts for scent

Instructions

Mix all ingredients except essential oils and extracts in a medium saucepan, stirring constantly over low heat. After a lumpy mixture forms, continue stirring until it forms a ball. Let the dough cool, then knead and mix in your scent. Store in sealed containers or zipper sandwich bags. Makes 2 cups.

Collect cookie cutters and other fun cutouts to enhance the play. Also, homemade Playdough makes an excellent and inexpensive gift. Wrap it in plastic bags and tie with curling ribbon. Other moms who need to get things done will thank you!

Slime Time

Good Buy **DIY** **Touch**

This is exactly as good and gross as it sounds.

Kids love gross stuff. It's just a fact! And what's grosser than slippery, sloppy, soupy slime? Kids can't keep themselves from squeeeeezing the stuff between their fingers and watching it drip and drop from their hands. And who can blame them? I bet you won't be able to resist trying it yourself. Slime is so mesmerizing that playing with it has become an online video sensation. Just watching people squeeze slime is enough to set some busy hands and minds at ease.

You can get slime pretty much anywhere that sells kids' stuff, but you can also make it really easily at home. Little scientists will love to help!

Put some Stretchy String (page 29), plastic spiders, squeezy eyeballs, or whatever ick-factor toys you have lying around into the slime to make an extra-gross experience. Or create themed Slime Time slime, making special colors for holidays like Halloween. Or go extreme with gross themes like dog barf.

DIY Directions

Tip! Store Slime Time slime in an airtight container or bag so it doesn't get moldy.

What You'll Need
½ cup Elmer's glue
½ tablespoon baking soda
couple drops food coloring
    or water-soluble
    color tablet (optional)
3 tablespoons saline solution

Instructions
Pour the glue and baking soda into a bowl. Mix with a spatula until thoroughly combined. Add food coloring, if using. Add saline solution a little at a time while stirring. Don't add too much at once, or your mixture will become hard. Smooth out lumps and add more saline solution if the slime feels sticky. Knead the slime until it feels slime-ish.

ENGROSSINGLY GROSS & MESMERIZINGLY MESSY

Recommended Reading

There are so many great books out there filled with ideas for projects to do with kids, advice on parenting, and stories that will keep kids absolutely mesmerized. Sometimes the best Fidget Buster is a great book! Here are some of my all-time favorite kid and kid-related books.

DIY Projects
The Little Hands Art Book
   by Judy Press

The Preschooler's Busy Book
   by Trish Kuffner

Parenting
The 5 Love Languages of Children
   by Gary Chapman and
   Ross Campbell

Siblings Without Rivalry by Adele
   Faber and Elaine Mazlish

Activity Book
Wreck This Journal by Keri Smith

Reference Book
Tell Me Why by Arkady Leokum

Story Books
The Oak Inside the Acorn
   by Max Lucado

Froggy book series
   by Jonathan London

The Best-Loved Doll
   by Rebecca Caudill

A Pocket for Corduroy
   by Don Freeman

Where the Sidewalk Ends
   by Shel Silverstein

Walter the Farting Dog
   by William Kotzwinkle and
   Glenn Murray

The Snowy Day by Ezra Jack Keats

*Chicken Soup with Rice: A Book
   of Months* by Maurice Sendak

Caps for Sale by Esphyr
   Slobodkina

Are You My Mother? P. D.
   Eastman

Lily's Purple Plastic Purse
   by Kevin Henkes

The Giving Tree by Shel
   Silverstein

The Very Hungry Caterpillar
   by Eric Carle

Big by Keith Haring

Arthur book series by Marc
   Brown

Pinkalicious book series
   by Victoria Kann

Fancy Nancy book series by Jane O'Connor

Guess How Much I Love You by Sam McBratney

Incredible You! by Dr. Wayne W. Dyer

Chicka Chicka Boom Boom by Bill Martin Jr. and John Archambault

Duck & Goose by Tad Hills

Duck in the Truck by Jez Alborough

Frog and Toad book series by Arnold Lobel

Olivia books series by Ian Falconer

You Are Special by Max Lucado

The Mitten by Jan Brett

Series for Older Kids
Harry Potter by J. K. Rowling

A Series of Unfortunate Events by Lemony Snicket

About the Author

Fast track to fun! It started out with her black bag of tricks— fun things to make to keep about 20 nieces and nephews happily busy at Grandma's house. Three daughters later, it grew to a full-fledged basement art room complete with everything ordinary to create something extraordinary—old record albums for penguin wings, spaghetti for a clown's hair, baby food jars for tornadoes. Now, parenting expert Donna Bozzo shares her ideas for simple, fantastic family fun on TV shows across the country, and as a *Today Show* contributor showing us easy-peasy ways to put more joy into our families' days. Donna has written for *Family Circle*, *American Baby*, *Working Mother*, and *Brides* and has worked as a TV producer, talk show host, and reporter—but her favorite job by far is M-O-M. Donna lives in Winnetka, Illinois, with her husband and three very fun, non-eye-rolling teenage daughters.

Fidget Busters is Donna's second book.

Index

Image Credits

Page 16: Joe Lops © Countryman Press (ball); page 22: © Donna Bozzo (goo bag); page 47: William Warby (tangle toy); all other images from iStockPhoto.com: Background page 1 and elsewhere: © gn8; background page 2 and elsewhere: © mydoc3737; sticky notes throughout: © subjug; check mark icon throughout: ©PeterPal; ear, eye, and hand icons throughout: © Obaba; scissor icon throughout: © browndogstudios; brain icon throughout: © IconicBestiary; page 10: © winnieapple (beads), © AntiMartina (marbles); pages 10 and 17: © JordiDelgado (rubber bands); pages 10 and 31: © SomeSense (colored sticks); pages 11 and 12: © Jamakosy (fidget spinners); pages 11 and 18: © happyfoto (baloons); pages 11 and 25: © SilviaJansen (yarn); page 13: © Alina555 (marbles); pages 14, 23, 26, 63: © krusunshiro (beads); pages 17, 28: © mrgao (scissors); page 19: © ansonsaw (rice); © soleg (funnel); page 20: © aroax (balloons); © ykbhat (ball); page 21: © happyfoto (balloons); page 23:

793 BOZZO

Bozzo, Donna.
Fidget busters

FAIRBRN

R4003419363

Atlanta-Fulton Public Library